101 Things® To Do With Tots

101 Things® To Do With Tots

BY
DONNA KELLY AND
TONI PATRICK

GIBBS SMITH
TO ENRICH AND INSPIRE HUMANKIND

First Edition
23 22 21 20 19   5 4 3 2 1

Published by
Gibbs Smith
P.O. Box 667
Layton, Utah 84041

1.800.835.4993 orders
www.gibbs-smith.com

Designed by Virginia Snow
Printed and bound in Korea
Gibbs Smith books are printed on either recycled, 100% post-consumer
waste, FSC-certified papers or on paper produced from sustainable PEFC-
certified forest/controlled wood source. Learn more at www.pefc.org.

Library of Congress Control Number: 2018966673
ISBN: 978-1-4236-5157-4

This book is dedicated
to home cooks everywhere
who strive to feed their families
flavorful and festive food.

www.gibbs-smith.com

CONTENTS

Side Dishes

Irish Boxty Potato Cakes 66 • Tater Bundt Cake 67 • Croquettes 68 • Asian Fried Tot Rice 69 • Creamy Sprouts and Tots 70 • Loaded Tots 71 • Tot Funeral Potatoes 72 • Denver-Style Tots 73 • Tot Poutine 74 • Mac and Cheese Tots 75 • Duchess-Style Tots 76 • Tot Pilaf 77 • Garlic-Parmesan Tot Fritters 78

Weeknight Dinners

Chicken Salsa Verde Tot Casserole 80 • Sheet Pan Chicken, Green Beans, and Tots 81 • Chicken Caprese Casserole 82 • Tot Crusted Fish Fillets 83 • Chicken Enchilada Tot Casserole 84 • Chicken Alfredo Tots Bake 85 • Chicken Curry Casserole 86 • Smoked Paprika Chicken and Tots 87 • Tot Seafood Paella 88 • Cod Tot Cakes 89 • Shrimp Scampi Tots 90 • Noodle-Free Tuna Casserole 91 • Chicken Broccoli Casserole 92 • Chicken Tot Pie Skillet 93 • Sheet Pan Sausage, Peppers, and Tots 94 • Sloppy Joe Tot Skillet 95 • Chili Cheese Bake 96 • Midwest Tot Hotdish 97 • Tot Crust Pizzas 98 • Cheeseburger Tot Cups 99 • Totsagna 100 • Tot Skillet Tamale Pie 101 • Tot Meatloaf 102 • Meatball and Tot Stroganoff 103 • Green Eggs and Ham Tots 104 • Cajun Tot Jambalaya 105 • Bierock Tot Casserole 106 • Shepherd's Pie 107

Vegetarian Meals

Vegan Buddha Bowl with Tots 110 • Tot Veggie Burgers 111 • Green Chile Corn Casserole 112 • Spinach Feta Tot Bake 113 • Stuffed Bell Peppers 114 • Swiss Veggie Tot Bake 115 • Persian Lentils and Tots 116 • Marinara, Mozzarella, and Tots 117 • Eggs Florentine Casserole 118 • Black Bean Tot Chilaquiles 119 • Mushrooms and Greens Casserole 120 • Greek Zucchini, Eggs, and Tots 121

HELPFUL HINTS

1. Tots are an excellent shortcut for busy home cooks. They come already cooked and often reduce cooking times for dishes. The recipes in this book are designed to take advantage of the convenience of tots by using them for chunks of potatoes in recipes.

2. There is no need to grate or dice potatoes, because smashing thawed tots will make them into small bits very quickly.

3. One 32-ounce bag of frozen tots equals about 8 cups of tots.

4. Some recipes call for using frozen tots, and others require thawed tots. To thaw tots, we recommend one of three methods.
- Place a bag of frozen tots in the refrigerator and let thaw for at least 8 hours and up to 24 hours.
- Spread frozen tots on a baking sheet in a single layer. Let sit at room temperature on the counter for 30 minutes.
- Place frozen tots in a glass bowl and microwave for 90 seconds. Stir and microwave again for another 90 seconds. Repeat this process until tots are thawed.

5. For deep frying tots, to see if oil is hot enough, dip the end of a wooden spoon into the oil. If it starts bubbling around the handle, the oil is hot enough to fry.

6. Tots made with vegetables other than potatoes can be found in most grocery stores. This book uses potato tots, but feel free to experiment with other tot varieties.

APPETIZERS & SNACKS

WAFFLED TOTS

4 cups **frozen potato tots**
ketchup, for dipping

Heat a standard-size waffle iron to high heat. Spread about 1 cup
frozen tots into the wells of the waffle iron, leaving a little space
between the tots. Lower the lid, leaving it slightly ajar—the lid will not
close all the way. Let cook for 2 minutes.

Carefully press down on the lid until it closes completely, gently
smashing the tots. Continue cooking for 3–5 minutes, until browned
and crispy. Repeat until all tots are cooked. Serve with ketchup.
Makes 4–5 servings.

BUFFALO TOTS

$1/2$ cup	**cayenne pepper sauce**
4 tablespoons	**butter,** melted
2 tablespoons	**brown sugar**
4 cups	**frozen potato tots**
$1/2$ cup	**blue cheese dressing,** for dipping

Preheat oven to 450 degrees. Prepare a baking sheet with nonstick cooking spray.

In a medium bowl, whisk together the pepper sauce, butter, and brown sugar. Add the tots and toss to coat.

Spread the tots in a single layer on baking sheet. Bake for 15 minutes. Remove from oven and turn tots over with a spatula. Bake for another 15–20 minutes, until tots are browned. Serve immediately with dressing. Makes 4–6 servings.

JALAPENO POPPER TOTS

24	**frozen potato tots**
4 ounces	**cream cheese,** chilled
1	**large jalapeno pepper***
1 tablespoon	**butter,** melted
1 tablespoon	**cayenne pepper sauce**

Let tots sit on the counter for about 15 minutes so they are semi-thawed. Preheat oven to 425 degrees. Prepare a baking sheet with nonstick cooking spray.

Cut each tot lengthwise, but not all the way through, leaving intact at the bottom. Place cut side up on the baking sheet. Place 1 generous teaspoon of cream cheese into the slit of each tot.

Cut the jalapeno in half lengthwise and then scoop out seeds and pulp with a spoon. Cut into 1/4-inch-thick half-moon slices. Place 1 jalapeno slice on top of the cream cheese in each tot, pressing down so that the jalapeno is embedded in the cream cheese, but still visible.

Stir together the butter and cayenne pepper sauce and brush over tots. Bake at top of oven for 15 minutes. Serve warm. Makes 4–6 servings.

* Wear plastic gloves to prevent negative skin reactions while cutting and seeding jalapeno pepper.

BBQ BACON BITES

18 slices **bacon**
36 **frozen potato tots,** thawed
1 cup **barbecue sauce**

Preheat oven to 400 degrees.

Lay bacon slices on a baking sheet in a single layer. Bake for about 15 minutes, until cooked through but not yet crispy. Remove bacon from oven, let cool a few minutes, and pat dry with paper towels. Cut each piece of bacon in half across the middle.

Wrap 1 slice of bacon around each tot and secure with a toothpick. Brush bacon-wrapped tots with the barbecue sauce, arrange on a second baking sheet, and bake for 15 minutes. Remove from oven and brush each tot again with barbecue sauce. Serve warm. Makes 4–6 servings.

BACON-DUSTED TOTS

20	**frozen potato tots**
3 strips	**bacon**
	ranch dressing, for dipping

Preheat oven to 350 degrees. Prepare a large baking sheet with nonstick cooking spray.

Place tots on baking sheet. Line a smaller baking sheet with parchment paper and arrange bacon strips on top. Bake tots and bacon for 20–25 minutes, turning the bacon occasionally, until bacon is crispy and dry and tots are golden brown. The bacon will probably cook faster, so keep watch to make sure it doesn't burn. When the bacon is done, remove to a paper towel–lined plate and cool completely.

Crumble the cooled bacon, place in a food processor or a high-powered blender and pulverize to a fine powder. When ready to serve, place the warm tots on a plate and sprinkle with bacon dust. Serve with ranch dressing on the side. Makes 2–4 servings.

PARMESAN AND GARLIC TOTS

1 whole head	**garlic**
1 tablespoon	**olive oil**
1 bag (32 ounces)	**frozen potato tots,** thawed
$1/4$ cup	**grated Parmesan cheese**
1	**egg,** lightly beaten
$1/2$ cup	**vegetable oil**
	marinara sauce, warmed, for dipping

Preheat oven to 350 degrees.

Cut the rooted top off the garlic head to expose the tops of the cloves inside. Drizzle olive oil over top and wrap in aluminum foil. Place on baking sheet and roast for 20 minutes, or until garlic is tender and lightly browned.

Place the tots in a large bowl and mash with a fork into small bits. Add the cheese and egg. Squeeze the roasted garlic from the skins into the bowl and mix until thoroughly combined. Using a spoon, scoop tot-size portions of the mixture into your hand and form back into tots.

Heat vegetable oil in a medium frying pan over medium heat. Working in batches, place formed tots into the hot oil and cook until golden brown on each side. Remove tots to a paper towel–lined plate. Cover to keep warm until all the tots are cooked. Serve warm with marinara on the side. Makes 8–10 servings.

REUBEN TOTS

1 cup	**sauerkraut,** drained
2 cups	**finely diced corned beef**
1 bag (32 ounces)	**frozen potato tots,** thawed and mashed
1 1/2 cups	**grated Swiss cheese**
1	**egg,** lightly beaten
1/3 cup	**breadcrumbs**
1 teaspoon	**garlic powder**
1 tablespoon	**dried parsley**
1/2 cup	**vegetable oil,** for frying
	Thousand Island dressing, for dipping

Press sauerkraut to remove as much moisture as possible and place in a large bowl. Add the corned beef, tots, cheese, egg, breadcrumbs, garlic powder, and parsley; mix thoroughly to combine. Using a spoon, scoop tot-size portions of the mixture into your hand and form back into firm tots.

Heat the oil in a medium frying pan over medium heat. Working in batches, place formed tots into the hot oil and cook until golden brown on each side. Remove tots to a paper towel–lined plate. Cover to keep warm until all the tots are cooked. Serve warm with dressing on the side. Makes 8–10 servings.

BACON-WRAPPED TOTS

Dipping Sauce

1/4 cup	**mayonnaise**
1/4 cup	**sour cream**
2 teaspoons	**brown sugar**
1 teaspoon	**red wine vinegar**
1 teaspoon	**oregano**
2 teaspoons	**cayenne pepper**

Tots

12 strips	**bacon**
24	**frozen potato tots**

Preheat oven to 450 degrees.

Dipping Sauce Place all of the dip ingredients in a small bowl and mix thoroughly to combine. Chill until ready to serve.

Tots Arrange a wire rack on a large baking sheet. Slice bacon strips in half lengthwise. Wrap 1 slice of bacon around each tot, securing with a toothpick if necessary and place on rack. Bake for about 25 minutes, or until bacon is crisp. Serve with dipping sauce. Makes 4–6 servings.

TOTS AU GRATIN WITH SOUR CREAM DIP

Sour Cream Dip

1/2 cup	**light sour cream**
1 tablespoon	**light mayonnaise**
1 teaspoon	**lemon juice**
1 teaspoon	**garlic salt**
1 1/2 tablespoons	**freeze-dried chives**

Tots Au Gratin

1 bag (32 ounces)	**frozen potato tots,** thawed
2 cups	**grated sharp cheddar cheese**
1	**egg,** lightly beaten
1/2 cup	**breadcrumbs**
1/2 cup	**vegetable oil,** for frying

Sour Cream Dip Combine all the dip ingredients in a small bowl. Mix thoroughly and refrigerate until ready to use.

Tots Au Gratin Place the tots in a large bowl and mash with a fork into small bits. Add the cheese and egg; mix thoroughly to combine. Using a spoon, scoop tot-size portions of the mixture into your hand and form back into firm tots. Roll tots in the breadcrumbs to cover completely.

Heat the oil in a medium frying pan over medium heat. Working in batches, place formed tots into the hot oil and cook until golden brown on each side. Remove tots to a paper towel–lined plate. Cover to keep warm until all the tots are cooked. Serve warm with Sour Cream Dip. Makes 8–10 servings.

ARANCINI DI PATATA NAPOLETANA

1 bag (32 ounces)	**frozen potato tots,** thawed
$1/2$ cup	**grated Parmesan cheese**
2	**eggs,** lightly beaten
$1/2$ cup	**breadcrumbs**
	salt and pepper, to taste
$1/2$ cup	**vegetable oil,** for frying

Place the tots in a large bowl and mash with a fork into small bits. Add the cheese, eggs, breadcrumbs, and salt and pepper; mix thoroughly to combine. Using a spoon, scoop tot-size portions of the mixture into your hand and form back into firm tots.

Heat the oil in a medium frying pan over medium heat. Working in batches, place formed tots into the hot oil and cook until golden brown on each side. Remove tots to a paper towel–lined plate. Cover to keep warm until all the tots are cooked. Makes 8–10 servings.

BROCCOLI CHEDDAR TOTS

1	**large head broccoli**
1 bag (32 ounces)	**frozen potato tots,** thawed
1 cup	**grated cheddar cheese**
1	**egg,** lightly beaten
	salt and pepper, to taste
1/2 cup	**vegetable oil,** for frying

Cut broccoli into small florets. In a steamer set over boiling water, steam broccoli until very soft. Drain water and set broccoli aside until cooled.

Place the broccoli and tots in a large bowl and mash with a fork into small bits. Add the cheese, egg, and salt and pepper; mix until thoroughly combined. Using a spoon, scoop tot-size portions of the mixture into your hand and form back into firm tots.

Heat the oil in a medium frying pan over medium heat. Working in batches, place formed tots into the hot oil and cook until golden brown on each side. Remove tots to a paper towel–lined plate. Cover to keep warm until all the tots are cooked. Makes 8–10 servings.

RED HOT TOTS

1 bag (32 ounces)	**frozen potato tots**
$^1/_3$ cup	**Frank's RedHot Sauce**
$^1/_4$ cup	**unsalted butter**
$^3/_4$ tablespoon	**white vinegar**
$^1/_8$ teaspoon	**Worcestershire sauce**
$^1/_8$ teaspoon	**cayenne pepper**
1 pinch	**garlic powder**
1 pinch	**paprika**
	ranch dressing, for dipping

Cook tots according to directions on the bag.

In a saucepan over medium heat, combine the hot sauce, butter, vinegar, Worcestershire sauce, cayenne, garlic powder, and paprika, whisking often. Once the sauce comes to a simmer, remove pan from the heat and allow to cool slightly. Sauce will thicken as it cools.

Place cooked tots in a large bowl and pour sauce over top; tossing to coat. Serve with ranch dressing. Makes 8–10 servings.

ASIAN-INSPIRED TOTS

Tots

I bag (32 ounces)	**frozen potato tots,** thawed
1/2 teaspoon	**onion powder**
1/2 teaspoon	**garlic powder**
1/2 teaspoon	**ground ginger**
	salt, to taste

Dipping Sauce

8 ounces	**grated sharp cheddar cheese**
I can (12 ounces)	**evaporated milk**
2 teaspoons	**red pepper flakes**
3 dashes	**soy sauce**
I tablespoon	**cornstarch**

Tots Cook tots according to package directions.

Combine onion powder, garlic powder, ginger, and salt in a small bowl; set aside.

Dipping Sauce Combine the cheese, milk, pepper flakes, and soy sauce in a saucepan. Cook over medium-low heat, stirring regularly. Once cheese has melted, slowly stir in cornstarch. Continue to cook, stirring constantly until sauce thickens; remove from heat.

Place cooked tots in a large bowl, sprinkle with reserved spice mixture and toss to coat. Serve immediately with cheese sauce for dipping. Makes 8–10 servings.

STUFFED CHEESY TOTS

Sour Cream, Onion, and Bacon Dip

I cup	**sour cream**
I	**green onion,** finely chopped
4 strips	**bacon,** cooked and crumbled
I teaspoon	**Sriracha sauce**
$^1/_2$ teaspoon	**Worcestershire sauce**
$^1/_2$ teaspoon	**salt**
$^1/_4$ teaspoon	**pepper**
$^1/_2$ teaspoon each	**onion powder and garlic powder**
I teaspoon	**sugar**

Stuffed Tots

I bag (32 ounces)	**frozen potato tots,** thawed
I teaspoon each	**garlic powder and onion powder**
I teaspoon	**salt**
I	**egg,** slightly beaten
12 ounces	**American cheese,** cut into small cubes
$^1/_2$ cup	**vegetable oil,** for frying

Sour Cream, Onion, and Bacon Dip In a medium bowl, combine all the dip ingredients and mix thoroughly. Chill until ready to serve.

Stuffed Tots Place the tots in a large bowl and mash with a fork into small bits. Add the garlic and onion powders, salt, and egg; mix thoroughly. Using a spoon, scoop tot-size portions of the mixture into your hand and form into a flat oval shape. Place I cube of cheese in the center of the oval and form mixture around cheese into a firm tot.

Heat the oil in a medium frying pan over medium heat. Working in batches, place formed tots into the hot oil and cook until golden brown on each side. Remove tots to a paper towel–lined plate. Serve warm with Sour Cream, Onion, and Bacon Dip. Makes 8–10 servings.

BLUE-BACON TOTS

I bag (32 ounces)	**frozen potato tots,** thawed
2 tablespoons	**all-purpose flour**
2 cloves	**garlic,** minced
I teaspoon	**salt**
$^1/_2$ teaspoon	**pepper**
6 strips	**bacon,** cooked and crumbled
$^3/_4$ cup	**crumbled blue cheese**
$^1/_2$ cup	**vegetable oil,** for frying

Place the tots in a large bowl and mash with a fork into small bits. Add the flour, garlic, salt, pepper, and bacon; mix thoroughly to combine. Using a spoon, scoop tot-size portions of the mixture into your hand and form into a flat oval shape. Place I teaspoon of cheese in the center of the oval and form mixture around cheese into a firm tot.

Heat the oil in a medium frying pan over medium heat. Working in batches, place formed tots into the hot oil and cook until golden brown on each side. Remove tots to a paper towel–lined plate. Cover to keep warm until all the tots are cooked. Makes 8–10 servings.

TOTCHOS

RED CHILI-
SMOTHERED TOTCHOS

I bag (32 ounces)	**frozen potato tots**
I pound	**lean ground beef**
I	**small onion,** chopped
I clove	**garlic,** chopped
I can (12 ounces)	**stewed tomatoes**
1 1/2 tablespoons	**chili powder**
1/2 teaspoon	**cumin**
1/2 teaspoon	**oregano**
1/2 teaspoon	**salt**
I can (14 ounces)	**kidney beans,** drained and rinsed
I cup	**grated cheddar cheese**

Cook tots according to package directions.

Cook ground beef, onion, and garlic in a large saucepan over medium-high heat until the meat is no longer pink and the onion is translucent. Drain off any grease and return mixture to the pan. Add the tomatoes and spices; stir to combine. Heat until mixture starts to bubble; reduce heat and simmer 5–10 minutes. Stir in beans and simmer until chili is heated through.

On a large serving platter, arrange half of the cooked tots, smother with half of the chili, and sprinkle with half of the cheese. Repeat with the remaining tots, chili, and cheese. Makes 8–10 servings.

CHICKEN, BACON, AND RANCH TOTCHOS

1 bag (32 ounces)	**frozen potato tots**
2	**frozen breaded chicken breasts**
8 strips	**bacon,** cooked crisp and crumbled
2 cups	**grated cheddar cheese**
	ranch dressing
1–2	**tomatoes,** diced

Preheat oven to 425 degrees. Prepare a baking sheet with nonstick cooking spray.

Place tots and chicken breasts on baking sheet and cook according to package directions. Check the chicken at 20 minutes; do not overcook. Remove tots and chicken from oven and reduce temperature to 350 degrees.

Arrange cooked tots in a large shallow baking dish. Dice the chicken and sprinkle over tots. Top with bacon and cheese; toss lightly. Bake for 5–10 minutes, or until cheese is melted. Remove from oven and lightly toss again. Drizzle dressing over top and sprinkle with tomatoes. Makes 8–10 servings.

BBQ PORK TOTCHOS

1 bag (32 ounces)	**frozen potato tots**
15 ounces	**smoked pulled pork,** warmed
1 cup	**barbecue sauce,** warmed
1 cup	**coleslaw**

Cook tots according to package directions.

Arrange cooked tots in a serving dish. Mix pork and barbecue sauce together and spread evenly over tots; top with coleslaw to serve. Makes 8–10 servings.

BLT TOTCHOS

1 bag (32 ounces)	**frozen potato tots**
18 strips	**bacon (about 1 pound)**
1–2	**tomatoes,** diced
2 cups	**shredded lettuce**
	squeezable mayonnaise

Preheat oven to 425 degrees. Prepare 2 baking sheets with nonstick cooking spray.

Arrange tots on 1 baking sheet and cook according to package directions.

Arrange bacon strips on the other baking sheet, making sure they don't overlap, and place in oven with tots. Cook bacon until crispy, 15–20 minutes depending on thickness. Remove from oven and drain on paper towels.

Arrange cooked tots in a serving dish. Crumble bacon and mix with tots. Top with tomatoes, lettuce, and a drizzle of mayonnaise; lightly toss and serve immediately. Makes 8–10 servings.

BEEF AND BEAN TOTCHOS

I bag (32 ounces)	**frozen potato tots**
2 pounds	**lean ground beef**
I	**small onion,** chopped
I packet (1.25 ounces)	**taco seasoning mix**
I can (14 ounces)	**black beans,** drained and rinsed
I–2	**jalapeno peppers,** seeds removed and sliced, optional
I cup	**grated cheddar or Mexican-blend cheese**
I	**tomato,** diced
I can (2.25 ounces)	**sliced black olives,** drained
	sour cream

Cook tots according to package directions. Remove from oven and reduce temperature to 350 degrees. Prepare a baking dish with nonstick cooking spray.

While tots are cooking, brown the beef and onion in a large frying pan over medium-high heat until the meat is no longer pink and the onion is translucent. Drain off any grease then return meat and onions to the pan. Add taco seasoning and mix well.

Arrange the tots in the baking dish and then sprinkle the beef and beans evenly over tots and top with jalapenos, if using, and cheese. Return to oven and bake 5–10 minutes, or until cheese is melted.

Top with tomato, olives, and dollops of sour cream to serve. Makes 8–10 servings.

CHICKEN FAJIT'CHOS

1 bag (32 ounces)	**frozen potato tots**
1 tablespoon	**olive oil**
2	**boneless, skinless chicken breasts**
1	**small onion,** sliced
1	**red bell pepper,** sliced
1	**yellow bell pepper,** sliced
1 cup	**water**
1 packet (1.25 ounces)	**fajita seasoning mix**
2 cups	**grated cheddar cheese**

Cook tots according to package directions.

In a large frying pan, heat oil over medium heat and cook chicken breasts until the meat is no longer pink. Cut chicken breasts in half and then into thin strips. Add chicken strips back to the pan along with the onion, bell peppers, and water. Stir in fajita mix. Heat until mixture starts to bubble and vegetables are done to your liking. Place tots on a serving platter and top with fajita mixture; sprinkle cheese over top to serve. Makes 8–10 servings.

GREEN CHILI AND CHEESE TOTCHOS

I bag (32 ounces)	**frozen potato tots**
2	**chicken breasts,** cooked and shredded
2 cups	**green chili,** warmed
I cup	**grated cheddar or Mexican-blend cheese**

Cook tots according to package directions. Remove from oven and reduce temperature to 350 degrees. Prepare a baking dish with nonstick cooking spray.

Arrange half of the cooked tots in the dish and cover with half of the chicken, half of the chili, and half of the cheese. Repeat for a second layer. Return to oven for 5–10 minutes, or until cheese is melted. Makes 8–10 servings.

BREAKFAST, BRUNCH & BITES

EGGS IN TOT NESTS

4 cups	**frozen potato tots,** thawed
1/2 cup	**grated cheddar cheese**
6	**eggs**
	salt and pepper, to taste

Preheat oven to 400 degrees. Prepare 6 (8-ounce) ramekins or 6 large muffin cups with nonstick cooking spray.

Place the tots in a medium bowl and smash with a fork into small bits. Press 1/3 cup of the smashed tots into each ramekin, covering the bottom and up the sides to form a crust. Bake for 15 minutes.

Remove from oven, sprinkle cheese evenly into the bottom of each crust, and crack 1 egg over cheese. Bake for another 5 minutes, or until egg yolks are cooked as desired. Let set for 5 minutes at room temperature.

To remove nests, slide a knife around the edges between the crust and the ramekins and carefully slide out onto plates. Season with salt and pepper. Makes 6 servings.

RANCH SKILLET BREAKFAST

2 tablespoons	**vegetable oil**
I	**bell pepper,** color of choice, diced
I	**medium onion,** diced
I cup	**diced cooked ham, or crumbled sausage, or crumbled bacon**
3 cups	**frozen potato tots,** thawed and cut in half
	6 eggs
	salt and pepper, to taste

Heat oil in a large frying pan on medium-high heat. Add bell pepper and onion and saute until softened and lightly browned, about 3 minutes. Stir in meat, cook for I minute, and then stir in the tots to combine.

Using the back of a large spoon, make 6 wells about $1/4$ cup in size in the tot mixture. Crack an egg into each well, turn off heat, and cover the pan. Let sit for about 3 minutes, or until egg yolks are cooked as desired. Season eggs with salt and pepper and serve immediately. Makes 6 servings.

CHORIZO-POTATO BREAKFAST BAKE

8 ounces	**uncooked chorizo,** without casings
$1/2$	**onion,** diced
6 cups	**frozen potato tots**
3	**green onions,** thinly sliced
I cup	**light sour cream**
8	**eggs,** divided
I cup	**grated cheddar cheese**
I cup	**grated Monterey Jack cheese**

Preheat oven to 400 degrees. Prepare a 9 x 13-inch baking dish with nonstick cooking spray.

In a large frying pan, cook chorizo over medium-high heat for a few minutes, breaking up into large crumbles. Add diced onion and cook another few minutes, stirring frequently, until onion is translucent. Remove from heat. Stir in the tots and green onions.

In a medium bowl, whisk together the sour cream, 2 eggs, and the cheeses. Stir into chorizo mixture and combine thoroughly. Spread mixture evenly into prepared dish.

Bake for 30 minutes. Remove from oven and make 6 evenly-spaced wells in the potato mixture with the back of a spoon. Crack I egg into each well. Return to oven and bake for another 5 minutes, or until egg yolks are cooked as desired. Let cool at room temperature for 5 minutes before serving. Makes 6 servings.

CHRISTMAS MORNING CASSEROLE

4 cups	**frozen potato tots**
6	**large eggs**
1 cup	**milk**
8 ounces	**cooked breakfast sausage links,** thinly sliced
2	**green onions,** thinly sliced, divided
1	**red bell pepper,** diced, divided*
1 cup	**grated cheddar cheese,** divided

Preheat oven to 400 degrees. Prepare a 9 x 13-inch baking dish with nonstick cooking spray.

Arrange tots in a single layer in the bottom of the dish.

In a large bowl, mix together the eggs, milk, sausage, most of the green onions, most of the bell pepper, and most of the cheese. Pour over the tots and scatter remaining green onions, bell pepper, and cheese on top. Bake for 35–40 minutes, or until set in the center. Makes 4–6 servings.

*For a more festive look, cut a few star shapes from the red bell pepper and scatter on top of casserole.

TOT CRUST QUICHE

4 cups	**frozen potato tots,** thawed
4	**eggs,** divided
1/2 cup	**all-purpose flour**
1 teaspoon	**salt,** divided
1 cup	**grated Swiss cheese**
1/2 cup	**diced onion**
1 cup	**diced ham**
1 cup	**chopped spinach**
1 cup	**half-and-half**
	dash of nutmeg

Preheat oven to 400 degrees. Prepare a deep-dish 9-inch pie pan or round cake pan with nonstick cooking spray.

Place tots in a medium bowl, and mash with a fork into small bits. Stir in 1 egg, flour, and 1/2 teaspoon salt; mix well to combine. Press potato mixture into the bottom and 2 inches up the sides of the pan. Bake for 20 minutes.

In a separate bowl, beat together the remaining eggs, and then stir in the cheese, onion, ham, spinach, half-and-half, and nutmeg; pour into tot crust. Bake 35–40 minutes, or until center is set. Let stand 5 minutes before serving. Makes 6–8 servings.

TEX-MEX TOT BURRITOS

2 cups	**frozen potato tots**
8 ounces	**uncooked Mexican chorizo,** without casings
6	**eggs**
1/2 cup	**milk**
2 cups	**grated pepper jack cheese**
6	**large flour tortillas**
	salsa, optional

Preheat oven to 425 degrees. Prepare a baking sheet with nonstick cooking spray.

Spread tots on a baking sheet and bake for 25 minutes.

While tots are baking, cook the chorizo in a frying pan over medium-high heat, breaking into bits as you cook it. (Note: If your chorizo is very lean, add a little vegetable oil to the pan before cooking.) Remove chorizo to a paper towel–lined plate.

Whisk together eggs and milk. Wipe out pan with a paper towel, and then cook eggs over medium heat until scrambled and cooked through.

Divide the chorizo, scrambled eggs, tots, and cheese evenly among the tortillas. Roll up burrito style, and serve with salsa. Makes 6 burritos.

TOT EGGS BENEDICT

4 cups	**frozen potato tots,** thawed
3	**egg yolks**
I tablespoon	**lemon juice**
1/2 teaspoon	**salt**
I dash	**cayenne pepper sauce**
10 tablespoons	**unsalted butter,** melted
4	**round slices of Canadian bacon**
4	**eggs,** poached or cooked to taste

Preheat oven to 425 degrees. Prepare 4 (8-ounce) ramekins or 4 large muffin cups with nonstick cooking spray.

In a medium bowl, smash tots into small bits using a fork. Evenly divide the tot bits into the ramekins, pressing into the bottom and up the sides to make a crust. Bake for 12 minutes or so, until browned and crispy.

Add egg yolks, lemon juice, salt, and cayenne pepper sauce to a blender. Blend for a second or two. With the blender running, slowly stream in the butter until sauce is thickened.

Carefully remove cooked tots from ramekins, keeping the round shape intact. Place on serving plates. Top each with a slice of Canadian bacon and an egg. Drizzle on sauce. Serve immediately. Makes 4 servings.

TOT HUEVOS RANCHEROS

1 can (14 ounces)	**diced tomatoes**
1 cup	**salsa**
1 can (14 ounces)	**pinto or black beans,** drained
4 cups	**frozen potato tots,** thawed
6	**eggs**
1 cup	**grated sharp cheddar cheese**

Heat a large frying pan to medium-high heat and add the tomatoes. Using a potato masher, mash until tomatoes are in small bits. Stir in salsa, beans, and tots. Simmer and stir until mixture is very thick.

Make 6 wells in the mixture with the back of a large spoon. Crack 1 egg into each well, cover pan, and cook until eggs are done to your liking, about 3 minutes. Sprinkle with cheese and serve immediately. Serves 6.

SCRAMBLED BREAKFAST BAKE

1 bag (32 ounce)	**frozen potato tots,** thawed
$1/2$ tablespoon	**vegetable oil**
6	**eggs**
$1/8$ teaspoon	**garlic salt**
$1/8$ teaspoon	**salt**
$1/8$ teaspoon	**pepper**
2 cups	**grated cheddar cheese,** divided
$3/4$ cup	**cooked, crumbled sausage**
$3/4$ cup	**cooked, crumbled bacon**

Preheat oven to 425 degrees. Prepare a 9 x 12-inch baking dish with nonstick cooking spray. Arrange tots along the bottom and up the sides of the dish. Bake for 15 minutes.

Heat the oil in a large frying pan over medium heat. Whisk together the eggs, garlic salt, salt, and pepper in a medium bowl. Pour eggs into frying pan and scramble until just set; do not overcook, the eggs will finish cooking in the oven.

Remove dish from the oven and use a spatula to slightly mash the tots into the bottom and sides of the dish. Sprinkle 1 cup of cheese evenly over the mashed tots. Layer the scrambled eggs over the cheese, and top with sausage and remaining 1 cup cheese. Sprinkle bacon over top. Place dish back into the oven and bake for 10 minutes, until cheese has melted and starts to bubble. Makes 6–8 servings.

ROSTI

6–8 tablespoons **salted butter,** melted, divided
I bag (32 ounces) **frozen potato tots,** thawed
salt and pepper, to taste

Preheat a large frying pan over medium to medium-high heat. Add
2 tablespoons of the melted butter.

In a large bowl, crumble tots and add 2 tablespoons butter; mix to
combine. Transfer mixture to frying pan and lightly press along the
bottom to form I large potato pancake. Cover, and cook for 6–8
minutes, or until edges begin to brown. Remove from heat.

Cover pan with a plate to flip the rosti out. Heat remaining butter in the
frying pan and slide the uncooked side of the rosti back into the pan.
Cover, and cook another 6–8 minutes.

Slide onto a plate and cut into wedges to serve. Makes 6–8 servings.

VARIATIONS: Add cooked and crumbled bacon, cheese, onions, fresh
herbs, or top each serving with a fried egg.

QUICHE CUPS

72	**frozen potato tots,** thawed
8	**eggs**
$3/4$ cup	**milk**
$3/4$ teaspoon	**salt**
$1/4$ teaspoon	**pepper**
I cup	**cooked diced ham**
3 tablespoons	**thinly sliced green onion**
I $1/2$ cups	**grated Swiss cheese,** divided

Preheat oven to 450 degrees. Prepare 12 standard-size muffin cups with nonstick cooking spray.

Place 6 tots in each cup and press into the bottom and up the sides to form a crust. Bake for 15 minutes and remove from oven.

Reduce oven temperature to 375 degrees.

In a medium bowl, whisk together the eggs, milk, salt, and pepper.

Divide the ham and onion evenly between the muffin cups and sprinkle 1 tablespoon of cheese over top. Pour egg mixture evenly into each cup and then top with remaining cheese.

Bake for 20–25 minutes, or until eggs are set. Test center with a toothpick to check for doneness. Allow to cool 5 minutes before serving. Makes 12 mini quiches.

LOADED POTATO CUPS

I bag (32 ounces)	**frozen potato tots,** thawed
$1/2$ cup	**butter,** melted, divided
I cup	**grated cheddar cheese**
8 strips	**bacon,** cooked and crumbled
I cup	**sour cream**
I	**fresh chive,** finely sliced

Preheat oven to 450 degrees. Prepare 16 standard-size muffin cups with nonstick cooking spray.

Place 6 tots in each muffin cup and press into the bottom and up the sides to form a crust. Bake until golden, about 20 minutes.

Fill each cup with $1/2$ tablespoon melted butter and I tablespoon cheese. Divide bacon crumbles evenly between the cups. Place under the broiler for about I minute, or until cheese has melted. Remove from oven and top with I tablespoon sour cream and a sprinkle of chive. Makes 16 potato cups.

MINI MEATLOAVES

68	**frozen potato tots,** thawed and divided
2 pounds	**ground beef**
2 tablespoons	**dried onion flakes**
4 tablespoons	**ketchup**
1 teaspoon	**garlic salt**
1 teaspoon	**onion powder**
1 teaspoon	**pepper**

Preheat oven to 350 degrees. Prepare 12 standard-size muffin cups with nonstick cooking spray.

In a medium bowl, mix together the beef, onion flakes, ketchup, garlic salt, onion powder, and pepper. Crumble 20 of the tots into the beef mixture, and mix well.

Lightly press 2 tots into the bottom of each muffin cup to form a crust. Divide beef mixture evenly between cups and gently press to mold into cup. Crumble 2 tots over the top of each cup.

Bake for 20–25 minutes, or until beef reaches 160 degrees and tots are golden. Makes 12.

CHICKEN AND BROCCOLI CHEDDAR CUPS

72 frozen **potato tots,** thawed
3 **chicken breasts,** cooked and diced
1 cup **grated cheddar cheese**
1 package (10 ounces) **broccoli in cheese sauce,** prepared according to package directions

Preheat oven to 450 degrees. Prepare 12 standard-size muffin cups with nonstick cooking spray.

Place 6 tots in each cup and press into the bottom and up the sides to form a crust. Bake for 15 minutes and remove from oven.

Reduce oven temperature to 375 degrees.

Portion chicken evenly between cups and top with 1 tablespoon cheese. Divide broccoli and cheese sauce evenly among cups. Bake for 20–25 minutes. Makes 12.

SALADS

WARM GERMAN TOT SALAD

6 strips	**bacon,** diced
1	**medium onion,** diced
2 stalks	**celery,** diced
1 tablespoon	**all-purpose flour**
1 tablespoon	**sugar**
1 teaspoon	**salt**
1 teaspoon	**pepper**
$^1/_2$ cup	**water**
$^1/_2$ cup	**apple cider vinegar**
1 teaspoon	**celery seeds**
4 cups	**frozen potato tots,** thawed

In a large frying pan over medium-high heat, cook bacon, onion, and celery until bacon is cooked through and vegetables are softened, 3–5 minutes. Stir in flour and sugar and cook for 1 minute. Add salt, pepper, water, vinegar, and celery seeds. Stir and cook until slightly thickened. Stir in tots and cook for about 2 minutes, until tots are hot. Serve immediately. Makes 4–6 servings.

SHORTCUT NICOISE SALAD

4 cups	**frozen potato tots**
1 cup	**trimmed and halved green beans**
4	**eggs**
$1/4$ cup	**olive oil**
2 tablespoons	**Dijon mustard**
2 tablespoons	**red wine vinegar**
1 teaspoon	**salt**
$1/2$ teaspoon	**pepper**
4 cups	**chopped romaine lettuce**
1 can (8 ounces)	**oil-packed canned tuna,** drained
2 cups	**cherry tomatoes,** halved
$1/4$ cup	**black olives,** sliced

Preheat oven to 425 degrees. Prepare a baking sheet with nonstick cooking spray.

Spread tots on baking sheet in a single layer. Bake for 15 minutes, remove from oven, and let cool.

Bring a medium saucepan of salted water to a boil over medium-high heat and cook green beans until crisp-tender, about 2 minutes. Remove beans with a slotted spoon, run under cold water, and set aside to dry. Return water to a boil and cook eggs for 8 minutes then drain and run under cold water. Peel eggs and quarter lengthwise. Let cool to room temperature.

Whisk oil, mustard, vinegar, salt, and pepper together in a large bowl. Add romaine and toss to combine. Spread coated lettuce on a large serving platter and top with tots, green beans, eggs, tuna, tomatoes, and olives. Serve immediately. Makes 4–6 servings.

ROASTED VEGGIE SALAD

4 cups	**frozen potato tots**
I cup	**diced sweet potato**
3	**small shallots,** quartered
8 ounces	**cremini mushrooms,** quartered
$^1/_2$ cup	**chopped walnuts**
$^1/_2$ cup	**extra virgin olive oil,** divided
2 teaspoons	**salt,** divided
I teaspoon	**pepper,** divided
$^1/_4$ cup	**red wine vinegar**
I tablespoon	**Dijon mustard**
2 cloves	**garlic**
$^1/_2$ cup	**crumbled feta cheese**

Preheat oven to 425 degrees. Prepare a baking sheet with nonstick cooking spray.

Scatter tots on baking sheet and bake 10 minutes.

Toss the sweet potato, shallots, mushrooms, and walnuts in 2 tablespoons of oil with I teaspoon salt and $^1/_2$ teaspoon pepper. Add the mixture to the tots on the baking sheet and return to oven to bake another 15 minutes, or until all veggies are fork-tender. Remove from oven and let cool.

Combine the vinegar, mustard, garlic, and remaining oil, salt, and pepper in a blender. Toss with vegetables. Scatter cheese on top and serve. Makes 4–6 servings.

ALL-AMERICAN TOT SALAD

8 cups	**frozen potato tots**
I cup	**diced celery**
$^1/_2$ cup	**finely diced dill pickles**
3	**cold hard-boiled eggs,** peeled and chopped
I cup	**mayonnaise**
2 tablespoons	**dill pickle brine**
I tablespoon	**sugar**

Preheat oven to 425 degrees. Prepare a baking sheet with nonstick cooking spray.

Scatter tots on baking sheet and bake for I5 minutes. Let cool and then chill in refrigerator for at least I hour. Cut each tot in half.

Place the chilled tots, celery, pickles, and eggs in a large mixing bowl. Whisk together the mayonnaise, pickle brine, and sugar then toss with the ingredients in the bowl. Serve immediately. Makes 4–6 servings.

TACO SALAD

I bag (32 ounces)	**potato tots**
I pound	**ground beef**
I	**small yellow onion,** diced
I packet (1.25 ounces)	**taco seasoning mix**
I head	**lettuce,** chopped
2	**tomatoes,** diced
3	**green onions,** sliced
2 cups	**grated cheddar cheese**
	Thousand Island dressing, to taste

Bake tots according to package directions; remove from oven and set aside.

In a large frying pan, cook the beef and onion over medium-high heat until beef is no longer pink and onion has softened. Stir in seasoning mix. Remove from heat.

In a large bowl, toss together the lettuce, tomatoes, green onions, and cheese until mixed. Add beef and tots. Serve with Thousand Island dressing. Makes 4–6 servings.

SOUPS

SHORTCUT LOADED TOT SOUP

4 cups **frozen potato tots,** divided
2 cups **warm milk**
1 1/2–2 cups **hot vegetable broth or water**
grated cheddar cheese, cooked
bacon bits, sliced green onions,
sour cream, for garnish

Preheat oven to 425 degrees. Prepare a baking sheet with nonstick cooking spray.

Spread tots out on baking sheet and bake for 20 minutes. Place 3 cups of the hot tots in a blender with the milk. Blend until very smooth, 60–90 seconds. While blender is running, slowly stream in broth until soup reaches the desired consistency. Smash the remaining tots with a fork and stir into the blender mixture.

Spoon into serving bowls and garnish as desired. Makes 4–6 servings.

SAUSAGE, KALE, AND TOT SOUP

8 ounces	**mild Italian sausage,** without casings
$^1/_2$	**onion,** diced
3 cloves	**garlic,** minced
4 cups	**chopped kale**
4 cups	**chicken broth**
4 cups	**water**
2 cups	**frozen potato tots,** thawed

In a stockpot, cook sausage over medium-high heat for about 5 minutes, breaking up into small bits as it cooks. Add onion and cook another 3 minutes, until softened. Add garlic and kale and cook another minute. Stir in broth and water, scraping up browned bits from the bottom of the pot. Bring to a simmer and cook about 20 minutes.

Stir in tots and simmer another 10 minutes, stirring occasionally. Serve warm. Makes 4–6 servings.

BROCCOLI CHEDDAR SOUP

2 tablespoons	**butter**
1	**medium onion,** diced
4 cups	**broccoli florets**
3 cups	**vegetable broth**
1 can (12 ounces)	**evaporated milk**
3 cups	**grated sharp cheddar cheese**
2 cups	**frozen potato tots,** thawed
a few dashes	**cayenne pepper sauce**

Heat a large stockpot to medium-high heat. Add butter and onion and saute for about 3 minutes. Add broccoli and cook another 2 minutes. Stir in broth and bring to a boil. Reduce heat and simmer for 10 minutes, until broccoli is softened.

Add milk, cheese, tots, and cayenne pepper sauce to the stockpot. Bring back to a simmer and cook another 10 minutes or so, stirring so that tots fall apart.

Scoop out about 1 cup of vegetables with a slotted spoon; dice and reserve. Use an immersion blender, or pour batches of mixture into a blender, making sure to fill the blender no more than halfway with each batch, and blend until very smooth. Add back into pot and stir in diced vegetables. Serve immediately. Makes 4–6 servings.

ITALIAN WEDDING TOT SOUP

8 ounces	**Italian sausage,** without casings, crumbled
1	**medium onion,** diced
3 cloves	**garlic,** minced
2 cups	**water**
1 can (15 ounces)	**great northern beans,** rinsed and drained
1 can (14 ounces)	**diced tomatoes,** undrained
1 can (14 ounces)	**low-sodium chicken broth**
4 cups	**frozen potato tots**
1 cup	**fresh spinach,** chopped
	Parmesan cheese, for garnish

In a large stockpot, cook sausage over medium heat until no longer pink. Add onion and saute until tender. Add garlic and saute 1 minute longer.

Add the water, beans, tomatoes, broth, tots, and spinach. Bring to a boil. Simmer, uncovered, until all vegetables are softened and tots are in small bits, 8–10 minutes. Serve with a sprinkle of Parmesan cheese. Makes 4–6 servings.

CLAM AND TOT CHOWDER

4 slices	**bacon,** diced
1	**onion,** diced
3 tablespoons	**all-purpose flour**
2 cups	**whole milk**
1 cup	**clam juice or fish stock**
1	**bay leaf**
4 cups	**frozen potato tots**
2 cans (6 ounces each)	**chopped clams,** with liquid
	salt and pepper, to taste
	diced parsley, for garnish, optional

In large stockpot or Dutch oven over medium-high heat, cook bacon until brown and crispy, 6–8 minutes. Transfer to a paper towel–lined plate, reserving 1 tablespoon excess fat in stockpot; set bacon aside.

Add onion to the stockpot and cook, stirring frequently, until translucent, 2–3 minutes.

Whisk in flour and cook until lightly browned, about 1 minute. Gradually whisk in milk, clam juice, and bay leaf. Cook, whisking constantly, until slightly thickened, 1–2 minutes. Stir in tots.

Bring to a boil, reduce heat, and simmer 10–12 minutes.

Stir in clams and liquid and cook until heated through, 1–2 minutes. Season with salt and pepper. If the soup is too thick, add more milk as needed until desired consistency is reached.

Serve immediately, garnished with bacon and parsley, if desired. Makes 4–6 servings.

EASY PEASY CORN CHOWDER

1	**large onion,** diced
2 tablespoons	**vegetable oil**
4 cups	**frozen potato tots**
4 cups	**low-sodium vegetable broth**
2 tablespoons	**all-purpose flour**
1 can (12 ounces)	**evaporated milk**
3 cups	**corn kernels**
1 cup	**grated white cheddar cheese**
	salt and pepper, to taste
1 tablespoon	**diced chives,** for garnish

In a stockpot over medium heat, saute onion in oil until translucent, about 3 minutes. Add tots and broth and bring to a boil. Reduce heat, cover, and simmer for about 10 minutes, stirring frequently.

Whisk flour into milk and stir into pot. Add corn and cheese and simmer until cheese is melted, 2–3 minutes.

Season with salt and pepper, garnish with chives, and serve. Makes 4–6 servings.

CROCK TOT SOUP

I bag (32 ounces)	**potato tots**
2 cups	**milk**
I can (10 ounces)	**condensed cream of mushroom soup**
I cup	**grated cheddar cheese**
I cup	**sour cream**
I cup	**chopped cooked ham**
$^1/_2$ cup	**finely chopped onion**
	salt and pepper, to taste

Combine tots, milk, soup, cheese, sour cream, ham, onion, and salt and pepper in a 4-quart slow cooker. Cook on high, stirring occasionally, for 4 hours, or on low for 5–7 hours. Makes 8 servings.

SIDE DISHES

IRISH BOXTY POTATO CAKES

2 cups	**flour**
I teaspoon	**baking powder**
I teaspoon	**salt**
I cup	**mashed potatoes**
20	**frozen potato tots,** thawed and crumbled
I cup	**buttermilk** (or more if needed)
	butter

Place the flour, baking powder, and salt in a small bowl, set aside.

In a large mixing bowl, combine the mashed potatoes with the crumbled tots. Stir in the flour mixture until well-combined. Slowly add the buttermilk and stir gently to form a thick batter.

Melt butter in a large frying pan over medium heat. Place about $1/2$ cup batter into the frying pan and flatten into a pancake shape. Fry until golden brown on both sides. Repeat until batter is gone, adding more butter as needed between frying. Makes about 12 potato cakes.

TATER BUNDT CAKE

2 tablespoons	**butter,** melted
2–3 cloves	**garlic,** minced
$1/2$–1 tablespoon	**Italian herb blend seasoning**
$1/4$ cup	**grated fresh Parmesan cheese**
2 cups	**grated mozzarella cheese**
3	**eggs,** beaten
	chopped fresh flat-leaf parsley, optional
1 bag (32 ounces)	**frozen potato tots,** thawed
	marinara sauce, warmed, optional

Preheat oven to 425 degrees. Prepare a Bundt pan with nonstick cooking spray.

In a large bowl, combine the butter, garlic, herb blend, cheeses, eggs, and parsley, if using. Add the tots and toss until well-coated. Pour tots into the Bundt pan, pressing so they will form into the bottom and sides. Bake for 30–35 minutes, or until crispy. Allow to cool 10–15 minutes, before inverting onto a serving plate. Cut into slices and serve with marinara on the side, if desired. Makes 8 servings.

CROQUETTES

I bag (32 ounces)	**frozen potato tots,** thawed
$^1/_2$ cup	**grated Parmesan cheese**
3	**eggs,** separated
	salt and pepper, to taste
I tablespoon	**dried parsley flakes**
I cup	**small cubes mozzarella cheese**
$^1/_2$ cup	**all-purpose flour**
$^1/_2$ cup	**breadcrumbs**
$^1/_2$ cup	**vegetable oil,** for frying

In a large bowl, mash tots with a fork into small bits. Add the Parmesan cheese, egg yolks, salt and pepper, and parsley; mix thoroughly to combine. Using a spoon, scoop tot-size portions of the mixture into your hand and form into flat oval shapes. Place about 2 mozzarella cubes (depending on the size) in the center of the ovals and form mixture around cheese into firm tots.

In a small shallow bowl, whip the egg whites together. Place the flour and breadcrumbs in separate shallow bowls. Roll each tot in the flour, then in egg whites, and lastly in the breadcrumbs.

Heat the oil in a medium frying pan over medium heat. Working in batches, place croquettes into the hot oil and cook until golden brown on each side. Remove to a paper towel-lined plate. Cover to keep warm until all the croquettes are cooked. Makes 8–10 servings.

ASIAN FRIED TOT RICE

3 tablespoons	**vegetable oil**
1	**large carrot,** peeled and minced
2 stalks	**celery,** minced
$^1/_2$	**onion,** minced
4 cups	**frozen potato tots,** thawed
2 tablespoons	**low-sodium soy sauce**
1 tablespoon	**honey**
1 teaspoon	**cayenne pepper sauce**

Heat a large frying pan or wok to medium-high heat. Add in oil, carrot, celery, and onion. Saute for 3–5 minutes, until softened.

Pulse the tots in a food processor until in very small bits the size of rice. Stir the tot bits into the pan. Continue to stir until heated through. In a small bowl, whisk together the soy sauce, honey, and cayenne pepper sauce. Drizzle over the skillet mixture, tossing until liquid is evenly distributed. Serve immediately. Makes 4–6 servings.

CREAMY SPROUTS AND TOTS

16 ounces (about 4 cups)	**Brussels sprouts,** grated
1	**large shallot,** diced
3 tablespoons	**olive oil**
1 1/2 cups	**sour cream**
1 1/2 cups	**grated Monterey jack cheese,** divided
4 cups	**frozen potato tots,** thawed

Preheat oven to 400 degrees.

In a large oven-proof frying pan over medium-high heat, saute sprouts and shallot in oil for about 5 minutes, stirring frequently. Turn off heat and stir in sour cream, most of the cheese, and tots. Sprinkle remaining cheese on top.

Bake for 18–20 minutes, until bubbly and browned. Makes 4–6 servings.

LOADED TOTS

4 cups	**frozen potato tots**
2 cups	**grated cheddar cheese**
1/4 cup	**diced cooked bacon**
1/2 cup	**sour cream**
3	**green onions,** thinly sliced

Preheat oven to 425 degrees. Prepare a baking sheet with nonstick cooking spray.

Spread tots in a single layer on the baking sheet, leaving space between tots, and bake for 20 minutes.

Remove tots from the oven and move them together in the center of baking sheet. Sprinkle cheese and bacon on top of tots. Bake for another 3 minutes.

Remove pan from the oven, drizzle sour cream on top of the tots, and sprinkle on green onions. Serve immediately. Makes 4–6 servings.

TOT FUNERAL POTATOES

1 cup	**sour cream**
2 cans (10 ounces each)	**condensed cream of chicken or celery soup**
2 cups	**grated cheddar cheese**
1/2 cup	**butter,** melted, divided
1 bag (32 ounces)	**frozen potato tots**
3	**green onions,** thinly sliced
1 1/2 cups	**crushed cornflakes**

Preheat oven to 375 degrees. Prepare a 9 x 13-inch baking dish with nonstick cooking spray.

In a large bowl, stir together the sour cream, soup, cheese, and half of the butter. Add tots and green onions and stir to coat.

Spread mixture evenly in the baking dish. Stir together the cornflakes and remaining butter and sprinkle on top of tot mixture.

Bake for 35–40 minutes, until bubbly and browned. Makes 6–8 servings.

DENVER-STYLE TOTS

4 cups	**frozen potato tots**
8 ounces	**thick-sliced ham,** diced
1	**green bell pepper,** diced
1	**onion,** diced
1 tablespoon	**olive oil**
2 cups	**grated Monterey Jack cheese**

Preheat oven to 375 degrees. Prepare a baking sheet with nonstick cooking spray.

Spread tots on baking sheet in a single layer and bake for 15 minutes.

In a medium bowl, toss together the ham, bell pepper, onion, and oil. Stir this mixture into the tots on the baking sheet. Bake for another 10 minutes. Remove from oven and stir in the cheese. Serve immediately. Makes 4–6 servings.

TOT POUTINE

I bag (32 ounces)	**frozen potato tots**
4 tablespoons	**butter**
4 tablespoons	**all-purpose flour**
2 cups	**beef stock or vegetable stock**
2 tablespoons	**soy sauce**
I tablespoon	**vinegar**
I tablespoon	**ketchup**
12 ounces	**cheddar cheese curds**

Preheat oven to 425 degrees. Prepare a 9 x 13-inch baking sheet with nonstick cooking spray.

Spread tots on the baking sheet. Bake for 25 minutes.

While the tots are cooking, make the gravy. In a large frying pan over medium-high heat, melt butter. Whisk in flour and cook for I minute. Whisk in stock and simmer for a few minutes, until thickened. Stir in soy sauce, vinegar, and ketchup.

Scoop tots onto serving plates and scatter cheese curds on top. Ladle hot gravy over tots and cheese and serve immediately. Makes 6–8 servings.

MAC AND CHEESE TOTS

I cup	**heavy cream**
2 tablespoons	**cream cheese,** cut into small chunks
2 teaspoons	**Dijon mustard**
2 cups	**grated sharp cheddar cheese,** divided
$^1/_2$ cup	**grated Parmesan cheese**
I teaspoon	**cayenne pepper sauce**
4 cups	**frozen potato tots**

Preheat oven to 375. Prepare an 8 x 10-inch baking dish with nonstick cooking spray.

Bring cream to a simmer in a large saucepan and whisk in cream cheese and mustard until smooth. Stir in I cup of cheddar cheese, Parmesan cheese, and cayenne pepper sauce until cheeses melt, 1–2 minutes. Remove from heat and stir in tots.

Spread evenly in the baking dish, top with the remaining cheddar cheese, and bake until browned and bubbly, about 30 minutes. Serve immediately. Makes 4–6 servings.

DUCHESS-STYLE TOTS

I bag (32 ounces)	**frozen potato tots,** thawed
8 cups	**boiling water**
I cup	**grated white cheddar cheese**
$1/2$ cup	**heavy cream**
$1/4$ teaspoon	**nutmeg**
$1/4$ teaspoon	**white pepper**
3	**eggs**
4 tablespoons	**butter,** melted

Preheat oven to 400 degrees. Line a baking sheet with parchment paper or a silicone mat.

In a large bowl, soak the tots in the water for I0 minutes. Drain well. Place tots in a food processor and process to a smooth puree, just a few seconds. Stir in cheese, cream, nutmeg, pepper, and eggs.

Scoop tot mixture, $1/4$ cup at a time, and place on the prepared baking sheet, pressing down slightly to form discs. (NOTE: for a more fancy presentation, use a large pastry bag with a large star tip to pipe $1/4$ cup mounds onto baking sheet.)

Brush tops of mounds with melted butter. Bake for 20–25 minutes, until golden brown on tops. Makes 4–6 servings.

TOT PILAF

¹/₃ cup	**slivered almonds**
I cup	**low-sodium vegetable broth**
3 tablespoons	**unsalted butter**
¹/₂ teaspoon	**garlic powder**
¹/₂ teaspoon	**ground black pepper**
¹/₄ teaspoon	**onion powder**
4 cups	**frozen potato tots,** thawed
I tablespoon	**chopped fresh parsley**

Heat almonds in a medium saucepan set over medium heat, stirring constantly, until they begin to brown and are fragrant, about 2 minutes. Add in broth, butter, garlic powder, pepper, and onion powder. Once the mixture starts to simmer, reduce to low heat.

Stir in tots, cover, and let cook for 2–3 minutes. Uncover and fluff with a fork. Serve, garnished with parsley. Makes 4–6 servings.

GARLIC-PARMESAN TOT FRITTERS

4 cups	**frozen potato tots,** thawed
3 cloves	**garlic,** minced
1/2 cup	**grated Parmesan cheese**
1	**egg**
1 cup	**panko breadcrumbs**
	vegetable oil, for frying
	dipping sauce, of choice

In a large bowl, smash the tots with a fork into small bits. Stir in the garlic, cheese, and egg. Scoop mixture into 2-tablespoon clumps and then smash slightly, forming discs about 1 inch thick. Spread breadcrumbs on a plate and then press each disc into the crumbs.

Heat a frying pan to medium heat. Add a little oil and place some of the discs into the pan, at least one inch apart. Cook for a few minutes on each side, until golden brown and crispy. Repeat until all of the fritters are done. Serve immediately with your favorite dipping sauce. Makes 4–6 servings.

WEEKNIGHT DINNERS

CHICKEN SALSA VERDE TOT CASSEROLE

3 cups	**1-inch pieces cooked chicken**
1 cup	**sour cream**
1 jar (16 ounces)	**chunky green salsa**
2 cups	**grated pepper jack cheese**
2 cups	**frozen potato tots,**
	thawed and divided
1/2 cup	**grated cheddar cheese**

Preheat oven to 400 degrees. Prepare a 9 x 13-inch baking dish with nonstick cooking spray.

In a large mixing bowl, stir together the chicken, sour cream, salsa, and pepper jack cheese. Gently stir in 1 cup of the tots. Spread mixture into the baking dish.

Place the remaining tots and cheddar cheese in a food processor and process into small bits. Sprinkle this mixture on top of the casserole and bake for 30 minutes. Makes 4–6 servings.

SHEET PAN CHICKEN, GREEN BEANS, AND TOTS

6	**chicken thighs,** bone in and skin on
4 tablespoons	**olive oil,** divided
I teaspoon	**salt**
I teaspoon	**pepper**
I tablespoon	**soy sauce**
I teaspoon	**Dijon mustard**
I6 ounces (about 2 cups)	**fresh green beans,** cut into 2-inch pieces
8 cloves	**garlic,** peeled and smashed slightly
4 cups	**frozen potato tots**

Preheat oven to 450 degrees. Prepare a large, rimmed baking sheet with nonstick cooking spray and heat in the oven for at least I0 minutes.

Brush the skin side of the chicken thighs with a little of the oil. Place chicken pieces skin side down on baking sheet and sprinkle the tops with salt and pepper. Bake for 20 minutes.

Whisk together the remaining oil, soy sauce, and mustard. Toss in the green beans and garlic. Remove pan from the oven, turn chicken over, and scatter the green bean mixture between the chicken pieces. Return to oven and bake another I0 minutes.

Remove from oven and scatter tots between the chicken pieces. Bake another I5 minutes. Serve immediately. Makes 6 servings.

CHICKEN CAPRESE CASSEROLE

4 cups	**frozen potato tots**
4 cups	**shredded cooked chicken**
1 jar (24 ounces)	**marinara sauce**
$1/2$ cup	**chopped basil leaves**
$1/2$ cup	**grated Parmesan cheese**
8 ounces	**mozzarella cheese,** sliced into $1/4$-inch-thick slices

Preheat oven to 375 degrees. Prepare a 9 x 13-inch baking dish with nonstick cooking spray.

Spread tots in a single layer in the baking dish. Layer the remaining ingredients on top of tots in the following order: chicken, marinara sauce, basil, Parmesan cheese, and mozzarella cheese slices.

Cover and bake for 40–50 minutes. Serve immediately. Makes 4–6 servings.

TOT CRUSTED FISH FILLETS

6 fillets (4–6 ounces each)	**skinless white fish,** such as cod, snapper, or tilapia
	salt and pepper, to taste
1/3 cup	**all-purpose flour**
2	**eggs,** beaten
1 cup	**frozen potato tots,** thawed
1/2 cup	**Parmesan cheese**

Preheat oven to 425 degrees. Prepare a baking sheet with nonstick cooking spray.

Pat fish dry and sprinkle with a little salt and pepper. Spread the flour on a small plate. Place eggs in a shallow bowl. Process the tots and the Parmesan cheese in a food processor into small bits. Spread this mixture onto a small plate.

Dip both sides of each fillet into the flour, then the eggs, and then the tot mixture, making sure the fillets are completely covered with the tot mixture.

Place baking sheet in oven and heat for 5 minutes. Place fish on baking sheet and bake for 20 minutes. Let sit 5 minutes before serving. Makes 6 servings.

CHICKEN ENCHILADA TOT CASSEROLE

2 tablespoons	**olive oil**
1	**medium onion,** diced
3 cloves	**garlic,** minced
2 tablespoons	**chili powder**
2 cans (14 ounces each)	**enchilada sauce**
3 tablespoons	**tomato paste**
4 cups	**cooked shredded chicken**
2 cups	**Mexican-blend grated cheese,** divided
3	**green onions,** thinly sliced
3 cups	**frozen potato tots**

Preheat oven to 400 degrees. Prepare a 9 x 13-inch baking dish with nonstick cooking spray.

Add oil to a large frying pan at medium-high heat. Add onion and saute for 3–5 minutes, until softened. Add in garlic and cook another minute. Stir in chili powder, enchilada sauce, and tomato paste. Cook for a few minutes, stirring until well-combined. Turn off heat and stir in chicken and half of cheese.

Spread mixture evenly in the baking dish. Sprinkle with remaining cheeses and green onions. Place tots on top, covering whole surface. Bake for 45–50 minutes, until bubbly and tots are browned. Makes 6–8 servings.

CHICKEN ALFREDO TOTS BAKE

1 jar (15 ounces)	**Alfredo sauce**
1/2 cup	**milk**
2 cups	**frozen potato tots,** thawed
2 cups	**uncooked cubed chicken breasts**
1 cup	**frozen peas**
1/2	**red bell pepper,** diced
1/2 cup	**sliced almonds,** divided
1/4 cup	**grated Parmesan cheese,** divided

Preheat oven to 350 degrees. Prepare a 9 x 13-inch baking dish with nonstick cooking spray.

In a large bowl, whisk together the Alfredo sauce and milk. Toss with the tots, chicken, peas, bell pepper, half of the almonds, and half of the cheese. Spread evenly in the baking dish. Sprinkle remaining almonds and cheese on top. Bake for 45–50 minutes. Makes 4–6 servings.

CHICKEN CURRY CASSEROLE

3 cups	**frozen potato tots**
2 cups	**chopped chicken breasts**
3	**green onions,** thinly sliced
$^1/_2$ cup	**sliced almonds**
I can (15 ounces)	**coconut milk**
2 cups	**light sour cream**
2 tablespoons	**lemon juice**
2 tablespoons	**curry powder**
2 cups	**grated cheddar cheese,** divided
$^1/_2$ cup	**grated Parmesan cheese**

Preheat oven to 350 degrees. Prepare a 9 x 13-inch baking dish with nonstick cooking spray.

Toss together the tots, chicken, green onions, and almonds and then spread evenly in the baking dish. Whisk together the coconut milk, sour cream, lemon juice, curry powder, half of the cheddar cheese, and the Parmesan cheese. Spread this mixture on top of tot mixture. Sprinkle remaining cheddar cheese on top. Bake for 45–50 minutes, until bubbly and browned on top. Makes 4–6 servings.

SMOKED PAPRIKA CHICKEN AND TOTS

2 tablespoons	**vegetable oil**
I bag (32 ounces)	**frozen potato tots**
I	**large sweet onion,** chopped
3 tablespoons	**unsalted butter,** softened
I	**large shallot,** minced
3 cloves	**garlic,** minced
2 teaspoons	**lemon zest**
$^1/_2$ teaspoon	**salt**
2 tablespoons	**smoked paprika,** divided
8	**chicken thighs,** bone in and skin on
3 tablespoons	**olive oil**
I tablespoon	**cornstarch mixed into $^1/_4$ cup of water**
	salt and pepper, to taste

Preheat oven to 350 degrees.

Brush vegetable oil in a large heavy Dutch oven or large cast iron skillet. Toss the tots and onion together and spread in Dutch oven.

Mix together the butter, shallot, garlic, lemon zest, salt, and I tablespoon of the paprika. Using your fingers, spread a heaping teaspoon of butter mixture under the skin of each chicken thigh. Place thighs on top of tot mix in Dutch oven, skin side up. Mix together the remaining paprika and the olive oil. Brush mixture on the chicken skin. Bake, uncovered, for 60 minutes.

Remove chicken and vegetables to a serving platter, reserving juices in the Dutch oven. Place Dutch oven on stovetop and turn on medium-high heat. Whisk in the cornstarch liquid and simmer until thickened. Season with salt and pepper. Drizzle sauce over the chicken and vegetables. Serve immediately. Makes 6–8 servings.

TOT SEAFOOD PAELLA

I bag (32 ounces)	**frozen potato tots**
3 cups	**seafood stock or chicken stock**
2 teaspoons	**turmeric**
2	**boneless, skinless chicken thighs**
	salt and pepper, to taste
3 tablespoons	**vegetable oil**
$^1/_2$	**red bell pepper,** diced
I cup	**frozen peas**
I pound	**frozen medium shrimp,** peeled and deveined, thawed
4 ounces	**cooked chorizo or Spanish Calabrese sausage,** sliced into $^1/_4$-inch-thick half moons

Preheat oven to 350 degrees.

In a large frying pan, simmer the tots, stock, and turmeric for 3–5 minutes. Turn off heat and let set for 5 minutes. Fluff with a fork so that the tots separate into small bits. Set aside.

Season the chicken with salt and pepper. In a small frying pan, cook the chicken in oil over medium-high heat until golden brown on both sides. Remove from heat and let cool to warm. Cut into bite-size pieces.

Stir the chicken pieces and all remaining ingredients into the tot mixture in the frying pan, reserving a few shrimp and sausage pieces to garnish the top before baking. Bake at top of oven for 20 minutes. Serve immediately. Makes 6–8 servings.

COD TOT CAKES

2 cups	**frozen potato tots,** thawed
3 tablespoons	**butter**
16 ounces	**skinless cod fillets**
3 cloves	**garlic,** minced
2	**green onions,** minced
2 tablespoons	**lemon juice**
1 tablespoon	**cornstarch**
2	**eggs**
	vegetable oil, for frying
	tartar sauce, optional

Pulse the tots in a food processor until very small bits the size of rice. Place in a large bowl and set aside.

In a large frying pan, melt the butter over medium-high heat. Add fish fillets and cook for 3 minutes. Turn over and cook another 1–2 minutes, until cooked through. Add to bowl with tots.

Add garlic and onions to pan and cook for 1 minute. Add in lemon juice and scrape up browned bits from bottom of pan, cooking for about 2 minutes, until liquid evaporates. Add pan mixture to bowl and stir together, breaking up fish into small pieces. Add cornstarch and toss to incorporate. Stir in eggs.

Spray a large plate with cooking oil. Using a $^1/_2$ cup measure, scoop up some of the mixture and place on plate, flattening slightly, to make 6 mounds. Chill for at least 1 hour.

Heat a large frying pan to medium and add a $^1/_4$-inch layer of oil. Carefully add in 1 fish cake at a time. Cook for about 3 minutes, until browned. Carefully turn over, using two spatulas, one on top and one on bottom. Cook for another 1–2 minutes, until cooked through. Serve immediately with tartar sauce. Makes 6 cakes.

SHRIMP SCAMPI TOTS

3 cups	**frozen potato tots**
I pound	**medium shrimp,** shelled and deveined
2 tablespoons	**butter,** melted
$^1/_4$ teaspoon	**red pepper flakes**
3 cloves	**garlic,** minced
I tablespoon	**lemon zest**
I jar (15 ounces)	**Alfredo sauce**
$^1/_2$ cup	**light sour cream**
$^1/_2$ cup	**grated Parmesan cheese**
$^1/_4$ cup	**minced parsley**

Preheat oven to 400 degrees. Prepare a 9 x 13-inch baking dish with nonstick cooking spray.

Spread tots evenly in the baking dish. Stir together the shrimp, butter, red pepper flakes, garlic, and lemon zest. Scatter the shrimp mixture evenly over the top of the tots.

Whisk together the Alfredo sauce and sour cream. Pour evenly over top of shrimp. Cover with aluminum foil and bake 20 minutes. Mix the Parmesan cheese and parsley together. Uncover the casserole and sprinkle this mixture over the top. Bake, uncovered, for another 10 minutes, until bubbly. Serve immediately. Makes 4–6 servings.

NOODLE-FREE
TUNA CASSEROLE

4 tablespoons	**butter**
1/2 cup	**diced onion**
1/2 cup	**diced celery**
I cup	**diced cremini mushrooms**
2 tablespoons	**all-purpose flour**
I can (14 ounces)	**evaporated milk**
I can (12 ounces)	**tuna,** with liquid
4 cups	**frozen potato tots**
I cup	**grated Monterey Jack cheese**
I cup	**crushed potato chips**

Preheat oven to 400 degrees. Prepare a 9 x 13-inch baking dish with nonstick cooking spray.

Melt butter in a large frying pan over medium-high heat and add onion and celery. Saute until softened. Add mushrooms and cook until most of liquid has evaporated and mushrooms are softened. Stir in flour. Stir in milk and simmer until thickened, about 3 minutes.

Remove from heat and stir in tuna, tots, and cheese. Spread evenly in the baking dish. Scatter potato chips on top and bake, uncovered, for 25–30 minutes. Serve immediately. Makes 4–6 servings.

CHICKEN BROCCOLI CASSEROLE

3 cups	**frozen potato tots**
3 cups	**broccoli florets**
3 cups	**1-inch pieces cooked chicken**
2 cans (10 ounces each)	**condensed cream of chicken soup**
1 cup	**light sour cream**
1/2 cup	**water**
2 cups	**grated cheddar cheese**

Preheat oven to 350 degrees. Prepare a 9 x 13-inch baking dish with nonstick cooking spray.

Spread tots in the baking dish in a single layer. Cook the broccoli florets in a microwave oven on high for about 3 minutes, until broccoli is crisp-tender.

Stir together the broccoli, chicken, soup, sour cream, water, and cheese. Spread this mixture over the tots in dish. Bake for 45–50 minutes, until bubbly around edges and browned on top. Makes 4–6 servings.

CHICKEN TOT PIE SKILLET

4 tablespoons	**butter**
$^1/_2$	**onion,** diced
2 stalks	**celery,** diced
$^1/_3$ cup	**all-purpose flour**
3 cups	**chicken broth**
$^1/_2$ cup	**sour cream**
1 package (10 ounces)	**frozen diced carrots and peas**
$3^1/_2$ cups	**diced cooked chicken**
4 cups	**frozen potato tots**

In a large ovenproof frying pan over medium-high heat, melt butter and add in onion and celery. Saute for 3–5 minutes, until slightly softened. Stir in flour and cook 1 minute. Stir in broth and sour cream and bring to a simmer. Cook until thickened. Turn off heat.

Stir in frozen vegetables and chicken. Scatter tots on top in a single layer. Bake for 35–40 minutes, until bubbly around edges and tots are browned on top. Let stand for 5 minutes. Serve hot. Makes 6 servings.

SHEET PAN SAUSAGE, PEPPERS, AND TOTS

16 ounces	**fully cooked Kielbasa-style sausage**
2	**bell peppers,** color of choice
1	**medium onion**
$^1/_2$ cup	**Italian dressing**
4 cups	**frozen potato tots**

Preheat oven to 450 degrees. Prepare a baking sheet with nonstick cooking spray. Place baking sheet in oven and heat for 5 minutes.

Cut sausage into $^1/_2$-inch slices. Cut peppers in half and remove seeds, stem, and pulp. Cut peppers into $^1/_2$-inch strips. Peel and cut onion into $^1/_2$-inch slices, pole to pole. Toss sausage, peppers, and onion slices in Italian dressing and spread on baking sheet. Bake at top of oven for 10 minutes.

Remove from oven and stir. Scatter tots on top. Return to top of oven and bake another 15 minutes. Turn oven to broil for about 2 minutes to brown the tots, watching closely so as not to burn. Serve immediately. Makes 4–6 servings.

SLOPPY JOE TOT SKILLET

1 pound	**lean ground beef or turkey**
$^1/_2$	**onion,** finely diced
$^1/_2$	**bell pepper,** color of choice, finely diced
1 can (16 ounces)	**tomato sauce**
1 cup	**water**
1 cup	**ketchup**
2 tablespoons	**brown sugar**
2 tablespoons	**Worcestershire sauce**
1 teaspoon	**salt**
2 cups	**grated cheddar cheese,** divided
4 cups	**frozen potato tots**

Preheat oven to 450 degrees.

In a large ovenproof frying pan, saute the beef for about 3 minutes over medium-high heat, breaking into small bits while cooking. Stir in the onion and bell pepper and saute for another 2 minutes, stirring frequently. Stir in the tomato sauce, water, ketchup, brown sugar, Worcestershire sauce, and salt. Let simmer for about 5 minutes, stirring frequently. When mixture is thickened remove pan from heat.

Scatter half of the cheese on top of the skillet mixture. Arrange tots on top of cheese in a single layer. Sprinkle remaining cheese on top. Bake at top of oven for 30 minutes. Serve immediately. Makes 6 servings.

CHILI CHEESE BAKE

1/2	**onion,** diced
1/2	**green bell pepper,** diced
2 tablespoons	**vegetable oil**
I can (14 ounces)	**diced tomatoes,** drained
2 cans (14 ounces each)	**chili**
2 cups	**grated cheddar cheese,** divided
4 cups	**frozen potato tots**

Preheat oven to 425 degrees.

In a large ovenproof frying pan over medium-high heat, cook onion and bell pepper in oil for 2–3 minutes, until slightly softened. Turn off heat and stir in tomatoes, chili, and half of cheese. Scatter remaining cheese on top. Spread tots on top in a single layer. Bake for 30 minutes. Makes 4–6 servings.

MIDWEST TOT HOTDISH

I pound	**lean ground beef**
I	**medium onion,** diced
2 teaspoons	**seasoned salt**
3 tablespoons	**butter**
8 ounces	**cremini mushrooms,** diced
3 tablespoons	**all-purpose flour**
4 cups	**milk**
2 tablespoons	**soy sauce**
I bag (16 ounces)	**frozen whole green beans,** thawed
4 cups	**frozen potato tots**

Preheat oven to 425 degrees. Prepare a 9 x 13-inch baking dish with nonstick cooking spray.

In a large frying pan over medium-high heat, cook beef and onion until cooked through, about 3 minutes, breaking beef into small bits. Spread mixture into the baking dish.

Melt butter in pan and add mushrooms. Stir frequently and cook a few minutes until mushrooms are softened. Stir in flour until it disappears. Stir in milk and cook until bubbly and thickened. Stir in soy sauce and green beans. Spoon skillet mixture over the top of the beef mixture. Scatter tots on top.

Bake for about 50 minutes, until bubbly and tot tops are browned. Serve immediately. Makes 4–6 servings.

TOT CRUST PIZZAS

4 cups	**frozen potato tots,** thawed
1 cup	**egg whites** (whites from about 4 eggs)
1 cup	**grated mozzarella cheese**
2/3 cup	**marinara sauce,** divided
2 cups	**favorite pizza toppings, such as cheese, pepperoni, sliced olives, peppers, or onions**

Preheat oven to 425 degrees. Line a baking sheet with parchment paper and spray generously with nonstick cooking spray.

Pulse tots in a food processor into very small bits. You should have 3 cups of tot bits. Stir in egg whites and mozzarella cheese. Divide tot mixture in half and mound each half separately on baking sheet. Press each mound flat using the bottom of a measuring cup, forming 2 (8-inch) circles that are about 1/2 inch thick.

Bake crusts for 20 minutes. Remove from oven, and using a wide spatula or pancake turner, turn each crust over. Bake for another 20 minutes.

Spread half of the marinara sauce on top of each crust. Scatter pizza toppings on top. Place pizzas at top of oven and broil for about 2 minutes, until bubbly. Cut into wedges and serve immediately. Makes 2 (8-inch) pizzas.

CHEESEBURGER TOT CUPS

4 cups	**frozen potato tots,** thawed
I tablespoon	**cornstarch**
I	**egg**
I pound	**lean ground beef**
I teaspoon	**garlic powder**
I teaspoon	**salt**
I tablespoon	**Worcestershire sauce**
I cup	**grated cheddar cheese**
	ketchup and mustard, for drizzling
	sliced cherry tomatoes,
	pickle slices, thinly sliced
	onion, for garnish, optional

Preheat oven to 425 degrees. Prepare 6 (8-ounce) ramekins or 6 large muffin cups with nonstick cooking spray.

In a medium bowl, mash tots with a fork into small bits. Stir in cornstarch and egg. Press tot mixture into the ramekins. Bake for 15–18 minutes, until browned. Let set for 5 minutes then carefully remove tot cups from ramekins.

While cups are baking, cook the beef in a frying pan, breaking up into small bits, until cooked through. Stir in garlic powder, salt, Worcestershire sauce, and cheese. Spoon mixture into tot cups. Drizzle with ketchup and mustard and garnish as desired. Serve warm. Makes 6 servings.

TOTSAGNA

16 ounces	**mild Italian sausage,** without casings
1	**onion,** diced
1 jar (24 ounces)	**marinara sauce**
1 can (4 ounces)	**sliced black olives,** drained
1 container (16 ounces)	**cottage cheese,** divided
3 cups	**grated mozzarella cheese,** divided
1/2 cup	**grated Parmesan cheese,** divided
1 bag (32 ounces)	**frozen potato tots**

Preheat oven to 400 degrees. Prepare a 9 x 13-inch baking dish with nonstick cooking spray.

In a large frying pan over medium-high heat, cook sausage and onions until meat is cooked through and onions are softened. Turn off the heat and stir in marinara sauce and olives.

Spoon half of the mixture into the baking dish. Dollop half of the cottage cheese on top and swirl into the pan mixture, leaving large streaks of the cottage cheese. Do not blend in the cottage cheese. Sprinkle half of the grated cheeses on top. Spread half of tots on top, evenly spacing them out. Repeat this process once more with the pan mixture, cottage cheese, and grated cheeses, ending with a layer of tots on top.

Bake for 45–50 minutes, until bubbly and tots are browned. Makes 6–8 servings.

TOT SKILLET TAMALE PIE

1 pound	**lean ground beef or turkey**
$1/2$	**large onion,** diced
1 jar (16 ounces)	**salsa**
1 can (6 ounces)	**tomato paste**
1 tablespoon	**chili powder**
1 can (4 ounces)	**sliced black olives,** with liquid
1 cup	**fresh or frozen corn kernels**
2 cups	**grated cheddar cheese**
3 cups	**frozen potato tots**

Preheat oven to 425 degrees.

In a large ovenproof frying pan over medium-high heat, cook beef and onion until cooked through. Stir in salsa, tomato paste, and chili powder, reduce heat, and simmer for 10 minutes. Turn off heat and stir in olives and corn kernels.

Sprinkle cheese over top evenly. Place tots on top, covering entire surface. Bake for 35–40 minutes, until bubbly and tots are browned. Let stand for 10 minutes before serving. Makes 6–8 servings.

TOT MEATLOAF

$1/2$	**onion,** minced
2 stalks	**celery,** minced
2 tablespoons	**vegetable oil**
2	**eggs**
$1/4$ cup	**milk**
1 tablespoon	**Worcestershire sauce**
1 teaspoon	**each salt and pepper**
1 teaspoon	**cayenne pepper sauce**
2 cups	**frozen potato tots,** thawed
2 pounds	**lean ground beef**
$1/2$ cup	**ketchup**
$1/4$ cup	**brown sugar**
1 tablespoon	**vinegar**

Preheat oven to 350 degrees. Line a baking sheet with aluminum foil and spray with nonstick cooking spray.

In a medium frying pan, saute the onion and celery in oil over medium-high heat until softened, 3–5 minutes. Let cool.

Place the eggs, milk, Worcestershire sauce, salt, pepper, cayenne pepper sauce, and tots in a food processor and process until pureed. Empty into a large bowl.

Using hands, mix the beef into the onion mixture. Combine with the wet ingredients. Divide mixture in half and form 2 loaves on the baking sheet.

Combine the ketchup, brown sugar, and vinegar and brush on the loaves. Bake for 45 minutes. Remove from oven and brush with remaining ketchup mixture. Bake for 15 minutes. Let stand 10 minutes before slicing. Makes 6–8 servings.

MEATBALL AND TOT STROGANOFF

3 cups	**frozen potato tots**
I tablespoon	**vegetable oil**
$^1/_2$	**onion,** diced
8 ounces	**cremini mushrooms,** diced
2 cups	**milk**
2 cups	**light sour cream**
I tablespoon	**Worcestershire sauce**
$^1/_4$ cup	**water**
I tablespoon	**cornstarch**
3 cups	**frozen meatballs,** thawed

Preheat oven to 350 degrees. Prepare a 9 x 13-inch baking dish with nonstick cooking spray. Spread tots evenly in the baking dish.

Heat oil in a large frying pan over medium-high heat, add onion and cook for a few minutes. Add mushrooms and cook another 3–5 minutes, until vegetables are softened.

Whisk together the milk and sour cream and stir into pan, scraping up browned bits from the bottom of the pan. Stir together the Worcestershire sauce, water, and cornstarch. Stir into pan and cook, stirring constantly, another 2 minutes or so, until liquid has thickened slightly.

Cut meatballs into bite-size pieces. Stir into pan. Pour mixture over top of tots. Cover with aluminum foil and bake 35–40 minutes, until bubbling. Serve immediately. Makes 4–6 servings.

GREEN EGGS AND HAM TOTS

I cup	**heavy cream**
I cup	**chicken broth**
2	**eggs**
$^1/_2$ teaspoon	**salt**
$^1/_2$ teaspoon	**pepper**
$^1/_4$ teaspoon	**nutmeg**
$^3/_4$ cup	**grated Parmesan cheese,** divided
I cup	**diced ham**
8 ounces	**frozen spinach or other greens,** crumbled
2 cups	**grated Swiss or Gruyere cheese**
6 cups	**frozen potato tots**

Preheat oven to 350 degrees. Prepare a 9 x 13-inch baking dish with nonstick cooking spray.

Whisk together the cream, broth, eggs, salt, pepper, nutmeg, and $^1/_2$ cup of the Parmesan cheese in a large bowl. Stir in the ham, spinach, Swiss cheese, and tots.

Spoon the mixture into the baking dish, cover with aluminum foil, and bake for 40 minutes. Uncover and sprinkle remaining Parmesan cheese on top. Bake at top of oven for another 10 minutes, or until browned and bubbly. Let set for 10 minutes before serving. Makes 4–6 servings.

CAJUN TOT JAMBALAYA

2	**chicken thighs,** skin on and bone in
8 ounces	**andouille sausage,** sliced into thin half moons
$1/2$	**green bell pepper,** diced
1 stalk	**celery,** diced
$1/2$	**onion,** diced
1	**small jalapeno pepper,** seeded and minced
1 cup	**thinly sliced okra**
3 cloves	**garlic,** minced
1 can (6 ounces)	**tomato sauce**
1 cup	**chicken stock**
1 tablespoon	**Cajun seasoning**
1 tablespoon	**cayenne pepper sauce**
4 cups	**frozen potato tots,** thawed
$1/2$ pound	**medium shrimp,** peeled and deveined

Place the chicken thighs skin side down in a large frying pan and turn heat to medium. Cover and cook for about 5 minutes to let the fat render out. Turn chicken over and let cook another minute or two. Remove thighs to a plate and then add sausage, bell pepper, celery, onion, jalapeno pepper, and okra to the pan. Saute for 3–5 minutes, until vegetables are softened. Add garlic and cook another minute.

Whisk together tomato sauce, stock, Cajun seasoning, and cayenne pepper sauce. Stir into pan, scraping up browned bits from bottom of pan. Dice chicken thighs and stir into pan. Stir in tots. Cover and bring to a simmer. Stir to break up tots into bits. Let cook for a few minutes and stir again. Add in shrimp, cover pan, and turn off heat. Let set for a few minutes, until shrimp is cooked through. Serve immediately. Makes 4–6 servings.

BIEROCK TOT CASSEROLE

1 tablespoon	**vegetable oil**
1 1/2 pounds	**ground beef**
1	**large onion,** diced
1 small head	**cabbage,** cored and diced
1 tablespoon	**all-purpose flour**
3 tablespoons	**Worcestershire sauce**
3 tablespoons	**soy sauce**
6 ounces	**American cheese,** cubed
6 cups	**frozen potato tots**

Preheat oven to 425 degrees. Prepare a 9 x 13-inch baking dish with nonstick cooking spray.

In a large frying pan, heat oil and cook beef over medium-high heat for about 3 minutes, breaking up into small bits. Add in onion and cook another 2 minutes. Add in cabbage and cook another 5 minutes, stirring frequently, until cabbage is softened. Stir in flour until it disappears. Stir in Worcestershire sauce and soy sauce. Turn off heat and stir in cheese until melted.

Spoon mixture into the baking dish. Scatter tots on top. Cover and bake for 30 minutes. Uncover and put back in at top of oven. Turn oven to broil and cook, watching closely, until tots are browned. Serve immediately. Makes 4–6 servings.

SHEPHERD'S PIE

1 pound	**ground beef**
1	**medium onion,** chopped
1 clove	**garlic,** minced
$1/4$ teaspoon	**dried thyme**
2 tablespoons	**ketchup**
1 tablespoon	**flour**
$1/2$ cup	**water**
1 bag (10 ounces)	**frozen mixed vegetables**
	salt and pepper, to taste
4 cups	**potato tots,** thawed

Preheat oven to 425 degrees. Prepare an 8 x 8-inch baking dish with nonstick baking spray.

In a large frying pan, brown and break up the beef until no longer pink, 4–5 minutes. Add the onion and garlic; cook until softened, about 4 minutes. Stir in the thyme, ketchup, and flour until combined; add the water and vegetables. Cook until vegetables are warmed through and liquid has thickened, about 3 minutes. Season with salt and pepper.

Spoon beef mixture into the baking dish and crumble tots evenly over top. Bake until potatoes are lightly browned and filling is bubbly, 10–15 minutes. Makes 4–6 servings.

VEGETARIAN MEALS

VEGAN BUDDHA BOWL WITH TOTS

2 cups	**frozen potato tots**
1/2 cup	**green or brown lentils**
1 cup	**vegetable broth**
1/2 cup	**tahini**
1 teaspoon	**cayenne pepper sauce**
1 cup	**sliced almonds,** toasted
1	**ripe Haas avocado**
1 tablespoon	**lemon juice**
1 cup	**sliced cherry tomatoes**
1/2 cup	**chopped parsley**
1 can (15 ounces)	**black beans,** drained

Preheat oven to 425 degrees. Prepare a baking sheet with nonstick cooking spray.

Place tots on the baking sheet in a single layer. Bake for 20 minutes. Let cool until warm. Smash with a fork to small bits.

While tots are baking, bring lentils and broth to a boil. Reduce to a simmer and cook for 20–25 minutes, until tender. Drain and toss with tot bits. Divide this mixture evenly into 4 serving bowls.

Mix tahini and cayenne pepper sauce and drizzle over top of bowls. Sprinkle almond slices evenly over tops of all bowls. Cut avocado into 1/4-inch slices, toss with lemon juice, and arrange on 1/4 of the surface of each bowl. Arrange tomato slices over another 1/4 of each bowl. Arrange parsley over another 1/4, and arrange black beans over the remaining 1/4 surface of each bowl. Serve immediately. Makes 4 servings.

TOT VEGGIE BURGERS

2 tablespoons	**butter**
1/2	**onion,** diced
1/2 cup	**diced carrot**
8 ounces	**cremini mushrooms,** sliced
1 cup	**frozen potato tots,** thawed
1 cup	**cooked brown or green lentils**
1 cup	**oats**
2	**eggs**
1 tablespoon	**soy sauce**
	vegetable oil, for frying

Melt the butter and saute the onion and carrot in a large frying pan over medium-high heat until softened, about 3 minutes. Add in mushrooms and saute another 2 minutes or so, until mushrooms are softened. Place mixture in a food processor. Add in tots and lentils and pulse the mixture until everything is in small bits. Do not puree. Empty into a large bowl.

Pulse the oats in the food processor into very small bits. Stir the oats into the bowl mixture. Stir in the eggs and soy sauce. Let mixture set for about 10 minutes.

Heat the frying pan to medium-high heat. Add a little oil. Using a 1/2 cup measure, scoop out burger mixture into 4 mounds in the pan. Press the mounds flat to make patties, cover, and cook for a few minutes, until browned on bottom. Turn burgers over and brown on other side. Serve immediately. Makes 4 servings.

GREEN CHILE CORN CASSEROLE

¹/₄ cup	**cornmeal**
I can (14 ounces)	**evaporated milk**
I	**Anaheim chile,** diced
¹/₂	**large onion,** diced
I tablespoon	**vegetable oil**
4	**eggs,** beaten
I cup	**frozen potato tots,** thawed
I tablespoon	**sugar**
I tablespoon	**cayenne pepper sauce**
I teaspoon	**salt**
I teaspoon	**pepper**
2 cups	**frozen or fresh corn kernels**
2 cups	**grated sharp cheddar cheese**

Preheat oven to 375 degrees. Prepare a 5 x 8-inch or a 9 x 9-inch baking dish with nonstick cooking spray.

In a large mixing bowl, stir together the cornmeal and milk and set aside. In a frying pan over medium heat, saute chile and onion in oil until softened, 3–5 minutes. Add this mixture to the cornmeal and milk. Stir in eggs.

Smash tots with a fork into small bits and then stir into the bowl. Add sugar, cayenne pepper sauce, salt, pepper, corn, and cheese and stir to combine. Spread evenly in the baking dish. Bake for 40 minutes. Serve hot. Makes 4–6 servings.

SPINACH FETA TOT BAKE

4	**eggs**
I container (16 ounces)	**cottage cheese**
I package (10 ounces)	**frozen chopped spinach,** thawed and squeezed dry
4 cups	**frozen potato tots**
8 ounces	**feta cheese,** crumbled
I teaspoon	**nutmeg,** divided

Preheat oven to 350 degrees. Prepare a 9 x 13-inch baking dish with nonstick cooking spray.

Blend the eggs and cottage cheese in the blender until smooth. In a large bowl, toss the blender mixture with the spinach, tots, feta, and half of the nutmeg. Spoon this mixture into the baking dish. Sprinkle the rest of the nutmeg on top. Cover with aluminum foil and bake for 40 minutes. Uncover and broil, watching closely, for a few minutes to brown the top of the casserole. Serve immediately. Makes 4–6 servings.

STUFFED BELL PEPPERS

6	**bell peppers,** color of choice
2 cups	**frozen potato tots,** thawed
3	**green onions,** thinly sliced
I can (15 ounces)	**diced tomatoes,** drained
I cup	**fresh or frozen corn kernels**
I tablespoon	**vegetarian Worcestershire sauce**
2 cups	**grated Monterey Jack cheese,** divided

Preheat oven to 350 degrees. Prepare a baking dish with nonstick cooking spray.

Cut tops off the bell peppers and scoop out seeds and pulp. Place the peppers standing upright in a baking dish. (You may have to slice a little off the bottoms of the peppers to make sure they stand upright.)

In a large bowl, smash the tots into small bits the size of rice. Stir in the green onions, tomatoes, corn, Worcestershire sauce, and most of the cheese. Evenly divide this mixture between the peppers. Sprinkle reserved cheese on top.

Bake for 35–40 minutes, until browned on top. Serve immediately. Makes 6 servings.

SWISS VEGGIE TOT BAKE

16 ounces	**frozen broccoli, cauliflower, and carrot mix**
1 cup	**light sour cream**
2 cans (10 ounces each)	**condensed cream of celery soup**
2 cups	**frozen potato tots**
2 cups	**grated Swiss cheese,** divided
1 can (4 ounces)	**French-fried onions,** divided

Preheat oven to 350 degrees. Prepare a 9 x 13-inch baking dish with nonstick cooking spray.

Stir together the veggies, sour cream, soup, tots, half of the cheese, and half of the fried onions in a large bowl. Spread mixture evenly in the baking dish. Cover with aluminum foil and bake for 40 minutes. Uncover, sprinkle on remaining cheese and fried onions, and bake another 10 minutes at top of oven. Serve immediately. Makes 4–6 servings.

PERSIAN LENTILS AND TOTS

3 cloves	**garlic,** smashed
3	**bay leaves**
2 teaspoons	**cumin**
$^1/_4$ teaspoon	**coriander**
4 cups	**vegetable broth**
I cup	**brown or green lentils**
2 cups	**frozen potato tots,** thawed
I cup	**golden raisins**
I	**onion**
	vegetable oil, for frying
2	**green onions,** thinly sliced
$^1/_2$ cup	**diced pistachios**
	salt and pepper, to taste

Place the garlic, bay leaves, cumin, allspice, coriander, salt, pepper, vegetable broth, and lentils in a medium stockpot. Bring to a boil. Reduce to a simmer, cover, and simmer for about 20 minutes, until lentils are softened.

Stir in tots and raisins and let simmer another few minutes, breaking up tots with a spoon into small bits. Drain off most of the liquid. Cover and set aside.

Cut onion in half and then into $^1/_4$-inch slices from pole to pole. In a medium frying pan, heat about $^1/_2$ inch of oil to medium-high heat. Add one half of the onion slices and cook until browned and crispy, about 3 minutes, stirring frequently. Remove cooked slices from the pan and repeat for the remaining onion slices. Stir the fried onion, green onion, and pistachios into the tot mixture. Season with salt and pepper. Serve immediately. Makes 4–6 servings.

MARINARA, MOZZARELLA, AND TOTS

1/2	**onion,** diced
3 tablespoons	**olive oil**
6 cloves	**garlic,** minced
2 teaspoons	**Italian seasoning**
1 teaspoon	**salt**
Pinch of	**red pepper flakes**
1 can (28 ounces)	**crushed tomatoes**
1/4 cup	**minced basil leaves**
8 ounces	**fresh mozzarella cheese,** in cubes or balls the size of marbles
1/2 cup	**grated Parmesan cheese**
8 cups	**frozen potato tots**

Preheat oven to 350 degrees. Prepare a 9 x 13-inch baking dish with nonstick cooking spray.

In a large frying pan over medium-high heat, saute onion in oil for about 3 minutes, until softened. Add garlic, Italian seasoning, salt, and red pepper flakes and cook another minute. Add tomatoes and simmer for about 10 minutes, whisking frequently, until mixture has thickened.

Turn off heat and stir in basil, mozzarella cheese, Parmesan cheese, and tots. Spread mixture evenly in the baking dish, cover with aluminum foil, and bake for 40 minutes. Serve immediately. Makes 4–6 servings.

EGGS FLORENTINE CASSEROLE

2 tablespoons	**butter**
1	**large onion,** diced
1 cup	**mushrooms,** diced
1 package (10 ounces)	**frozen chopped spinach,** thawed and squeezed dry
4 cups	**frozen potato tots**
12	**eggs**
2 cups	**milk**
1 cup	**shredded Swiss cheese**
1 cup	**shredded sharp cheddar cheese**
1 teaspoon	**smoked paprika**

Preheat oven to 350 degrees. Prepare a 9 x 13-inch baking dish with nonstick cooking spray.

In a large frying pan, heat butter over medium-high heat. Add onion and saute 3–5 minutes or until softened. Add mushrooms and saute another 2 minutes. Stir in spinach and saute a minute or so, just until softened.

Spread tots evenly in the baking dish. Spoon pan mixture over tots.

In a large bowl, whisk eggs and milk until blended; pour egg mixture over vegetables. Sprinkle with cheeses and paprika. Bake, uncovered, for 35–45 minutes or until the center is set. Let stand 10 minutes before serving. Makes 4–6 servings.

BLACK BEAN TOT CHILAQUILES

2	**poblano peppers,** diced
1	**large onion,** diced
2 tablespoons	**vegetable oil**
2–3	**canned chipotle peppers in adobo sauce**
1 can (14 ounces)	**diced tomatoes,** with liquid
2 cans (14 ounces each)	**black beans,** with liquid
8 ounces	**pepper jack cheese,** grated
4 cups	**frozen potato tots**
8 ounces	**sharp cheddar cheese,** grated
2 cups	**crushed tortilla chips or corn chips**

Preheat oven to 425 degrees. Prepare a 9 x 13-inch baking dish with nonstick cooking spray.

In a large frying pan over medium high heat, saute poblano peppers and onion in oil for about 3 minutes. Smash chipotle peppers into small bits with a fork. Stir the peppers, diced tomatoes, black beans, and pepper jack cheese into the skillet.

Spread tots evenly in the baking dish. Spoon pan mixture over top of tots. Sprinkle cheddar cheese on top. Bake for 30 minutes. Scatter crushed chips on top and serve immediately. Makes 4–6 servings.

MUSHROOMS AND GREENS CASSEROLE

2 tablespoons	**olive oil**
I	**onion,** diced
2 pounds	**cremini mushrooms,** thinly sliced
3 cloves	**garlic,** minced
I tablespoon	**minced thyme leaves**
I can (28 ounces)	**diced tomatoes**
8 ounces	**kale, Swiss chard, or spinach,** chopped
4 cups	**frozen potato tots**
4 ounces	**fontina cheese,** grated

Preheat oven to 400 degrees. Prepare a 9 x 13-inch baking dish with nonstick cooking spray.

Heat oil in a large frying pan over medium-high heat. Add onion and saute for 3 minutes, or until softened. Add mushrooms and saute until browned and softened. Add garlic and thyme and cook another minute. Add tomatoes and simmer until liquid is almost gone, 8–10 minutes. Stir in greens and cook just until wilted.

Spread tots evenly in the baking dish. Spread pan mixture over top of tots. Sprinkle cheese on top. Bake for 25–30 minutes, until bubbly. Serve immediately. Makes 4–6 servings.

GREEK ZUCCHINI, EGGS, AND TOTS

3	**medium zucchini,** grated
1 teaspoon	**salt**
1 tablespoon	**olive oil**
6	**green onions,** thinly sliced
2 cloves	**garlic,** minced
6	**eggs**
1/2 cup	**milk**
1/2 teaspoon	**pepper**
4 ounces	**crumbled feta cheese**
1/4 cup	**chopped fresh dill**
4 cups	**frozen potato tots**

Preheat oven to 375 degrees. Prepare a 9 x 13-inch baking dish with nonstick cooking spray.

Toss zucchini in salt and let set for at least 10 minutes. Using a thin kitchen towel, squeeze zucchini over the sink until most of water has been extracted.

Heat the oil in a large frying pan over medium-high heat. Add green onions and garlic and cook until softened, about 2 minutes. Add in squeezed zucchini, cover, and cook about 3 minutes. Uncover and continue cooking, stirring constantly, until most of liquid has evaporated.

Beat eggs, milk, and pepper together with a fork in a large bowl. Stir in feta, dill, zucchini mixture, and tots. Spread the mixture evenly in the baking dish and bake for 25–30 minutes, until cooked through and edges are lightly browned. Let rest for 5 minutes before serving. Makes 4–6 servings.

NOTES

NOTES

NOTES

NOTES

NOTES

METRIC CONVERSION CHART

Volume Measurements

U.S.	Metric
1 teaspoon	5 ml
1 tablespoon	15 ml
1/4 cup	60 ml
1/3 cup	75 ml
1/2 cup	125 ml
2/3 cup	150 ml
3/4 cup	175 ml
1 cup	250 ml

Weight Measurements

U.S.	Metric
1/2 ounce	15 g
1 ounce	30 g
3 ounces	90 g
4 ounces	115 g
8 ounces	225 g
12 ounces	350 g
1 pound	450 g
2 1/4 pounds	1 kg

Temperature Conversion

Fahrenheit	Celsius
250	120
300	150
325	160
350	180
375	190
400	200
425	220
450	230

Yum! Check out these "101" favorites
for more tasty recipes:

Each 128 pages, $9.99

Available at bookstores or directly from GIBBS SMITH
1.800.835.4993
www.gibbs-smith.com

ABOUT THE AUTHORS

Donna Kelly, a food fanatic and recipe developer, is the author of several cookbooks including *French Toast, Quesadillas, 101 Things to Do with a Tortilla,* and *101 Things to Do with An Instant Pot*®. She lives in Salt Lake City, Utah.

Toni Patrick is the culinary creative behind the wildly successful *101 Things to Do with Ramen Noodles,* as well as several other titles in the popular 101 book series, including *101 Things to Do with Mac & Cheese,* and *101 More Things to Do with Ramen Noodles.* She has been featured on the Food Network, and lives in Greeley, Colorado.